Cursive Handwriting Workbook For Kids

Cursive for beginners workbook. Cursive letter tracing book. Cursive writing practice book to learn writing in cursive

This book belongs t

This is a beginning cursive handwriting book that helps kids learn cursive writing in a fun and easy way.

It is organized in a progressively skill building way to help kids develop confidence to write in cursive.

This book requires guidance from a teacher, parent or care giver to help the child practice cursive writing.

You can photocopy parts of this book for use with a family member.

However, teachers are not allowed to reproduce worksheets for other teachers or for entire school use. Please encourage other teachers to buy their own copy of this book!

Meet Jojo.
Jojo is a curious elephant.
He loves to learn and play.
Learn to write in cursive along with Jojo!

This Cursive Handwriting workbook is divided
into the following parts:

Part 1: Learning the Cursive Alphabet:
Trace and practice letters a-z and A-Z

Part 2: Writing two letter words:
Connecting lowercase cursive letters a-z

Part 3: Writing three letter words:
Connecting lowercase cursive letters a-z

Part 4: Writing four letter words
Connecting simple words

Part 5: Writing words starting with a Capital letter:
Connecting uppercase cursive letters A-Z

Part 6: Writing Numbers and Number Words 1-10
Learn and practice numbers 1-10

Part 7: Writing simple sentences
Connecting words to form an entire sentence.

Kids can use a pencil, light color marker or highlighter
to trace the dotted letters and words.

Hi!

My name is Sujatha Lalgudi. I sincerely hope you find my cursive handwriting book to be helpful and fun.

Write to me at **sujatha.lalgudi@gmail.com** with the subject:

Jojo Cursive along with **your kid's name** to receive:

- Additional practice worksheets.
- A name tracing worksheet so your kid can practice writing their own name.
- An Award Certificate in Color to gift your kid!

If you liked this book, please leave me a review on Amazon! Your kind reviews and comments will encourage me to make more books like this.

Thank you
Sujatha Lalgudi

Part 1:
Learning Letters

Trace the letters and practice writing them in the remaining space!

Color the picture and read the sight word out aloud.

Use the blank practice page to write on your own at the end.

Are you ready?
Let's go!

Name: _____   Date: _____

A is for

Alligator

Trace inside the cursive letter by following the arrows

Trace the cursive letters, then write your own.

Trace inside the cursive letter by following the arrows

Trace the cursive letters, then write your own.

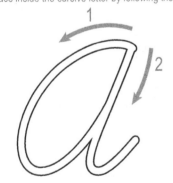

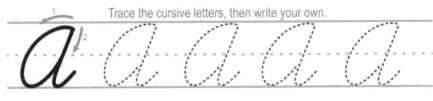

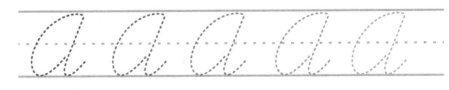

A B C D E F G H I J K L M N O P Q R S T U V W X Y Z

B is for

Bear

Trace inside the cursive letter by following the arrows

Trace the cursive letters, then write your own.

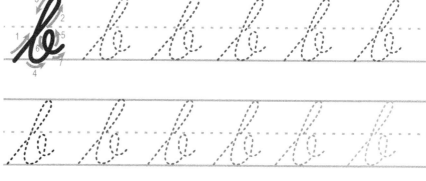

Trace inside the cursive letter by following the arrows

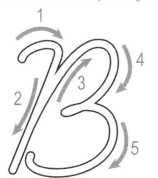

Trace the cursive letters, then write your own.

A **B** C D E F G H I J K L M N O P Q R S T U V W X Y Z

Name: _____ Date: _____

C is for Cheetah

Trace inside the cursive letter by following the arrows

Trace the cursive letters, then write your own.

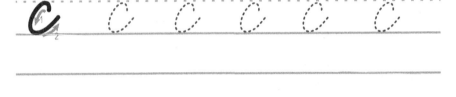

Trace inside the cursive letter by following the arrows

Trace the cursive letters, then write your own.

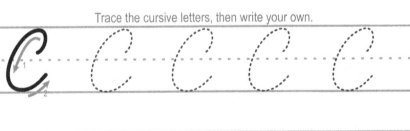

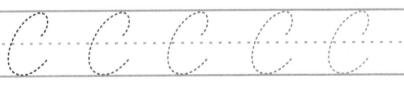

A B C D E F G H I J K L M N O P Q R S T U V W X Y Z

Name: _____ Date: _____

D is for

Dolphin

Trace inside the cursive letter by following the arrows

Trace the cursive letters, then write your own.

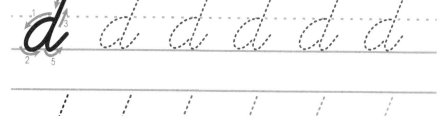

Trace inside the cursive letter by following the arrows

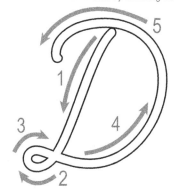

Trace the cursive letters, then write your own.

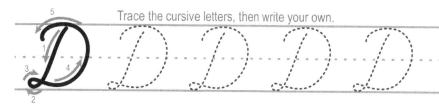

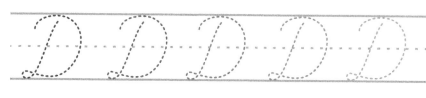

A B C D E F G H I J K L M N O P Q R S T U V W X Y Z

Name: _____   Date: _____

Trace inside the cursive letter by following the arrows

Trace the cursive letters, then write your own.

Trace inside the cursive letter by following the arrows

Trace the cursive letters, then write your own.

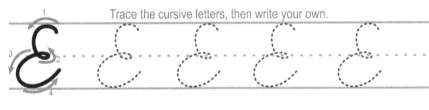

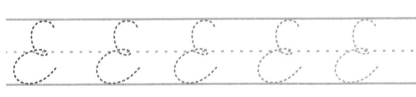

A B C D **E** F G H I J K L M N O P Q R S T U V W X Y Z

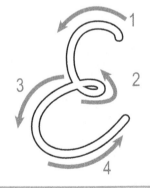

Name: _____ Date: _____

F is for Fox

Trace inside the cursive letter by following the arrows

Trace the cursive letters, then write your own.

f f f f f f

f f f f f f

f

Trace inside the cursive letter by following the arrows

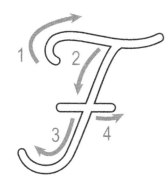

Trace the cursive letters, then write your own.

F F F F F

F F F F F

F

A B C D E **F** G H I J K L M N O P Q R S T U V W X Y Z

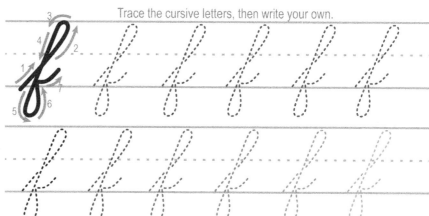

Name: _____   Date: _____

Trace inside the cursive letter by following the arrows

Trace the cursive letters, then write your own.

Trace inside the cursive letter by following the arrows

Trace the cursive letters, then write your own.

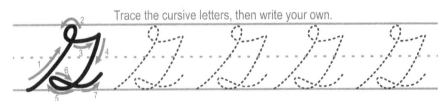

A B C D E F **G** H I J K L M N O P Q R S T U V W X Y Z

Name: _____   Date: _____

H is for

Horse

Trace inside the cursive letter by following the arrows

Trace the cursive letters, then write your own.

h h h h h h

h h h h h h

h

Trace inside the cursive letter by following the arrows

Trace the cursive letters, then write your own.

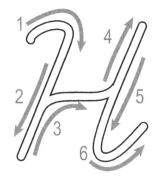

H H H H H

H H H H H

H

| A | B | C | D | E | F | G | H | I | J | K | L | M | N | O | P | Q | R | S | T | U | V | W | X | Y | Z |

Name: _____ Date: _____

I is for

Iguana

Trace inside the cursive letter by following the arrows

Trace the cursive letters, then write your own.

i *i* *i* *i* *i* *i*

i *i* *i* *i* *i* *i*

i

Trace inside the cursive letter by following the arrows

Trace the cursive letters, then write your own.

l *l* *l* *l* *l*

l *l* *l* *l* *l*

l

A B C D E F G H **I** J K L M N O P Q R S T U V W X Y Z

Name: _____   Date: _____

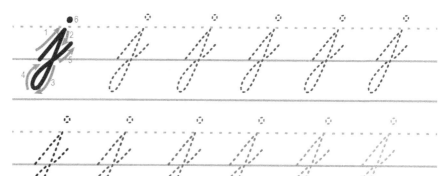

Trace inside the cursive letter by following the arrows

Trace the cursive letters, then write your own.

Trace inside the cursive letter by following the arrows

Trace the cursive letters, then write your own.

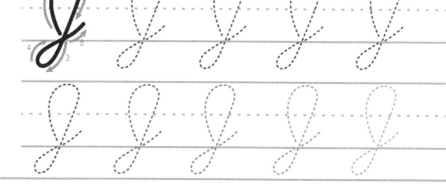

A B C D E F G H I **J** K L M N O P Q R S T U V W X Y Z

Name: _____   Date: _____

K is for

Kangaroo

Trace inside the cursive letter by following the arrows

Trace the cursive letters, then write your own.

Trace inside the cursive letter by following the arrows

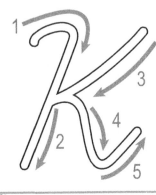

Trace the cursive letters, then write your own.

A B C D E F G H I J **K** L M N O P Q R S T U V W X Y Z

Name: _____ Date: _____

L is for

Lion

Trace inside the cursive letter by following the arrows

Trace the cursive letters, then write your own.

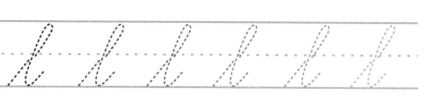

Trace inside the cursive letter by following the arrows

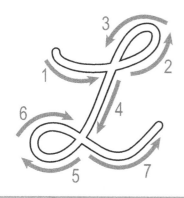

Trace the cursive letters, then write your own.

A B C D E F G H I J K **L** M N O P Q R S T U V W X Y Z

Name: _____ Date: _____

Trace inside the cursive letter by following the arrows

Trace the cursive letters, then write your own.

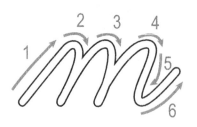

Trace inside the cursive letter by following the arrows

Trace the cursive letters, then write your own.

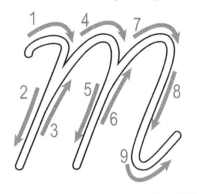

A B C D E F G H I J K L M N O P Q R S T U V W X Y Z

Name: _____   Date: _____

N is for
Narwhal

Trace inside the cursive letter by following the arrows

Trace the cursive letters, then write your own.

𝓃 𝓃 𝓃 𝓃 𝓃 𝓃

𝓃 𝓃 𝓃 𝓃 𝓃 𝓃

𝓃

Trace inside the cursive letter by following the arrows

Trace the cursive letters, then write your own.

𝓝 𝓝 𝓝 𝓝 𝓝

𝓝 𝓝 𝓝 𝓝 𝓝

𝓝

A B C D E F G H I J K L M **N** O P Q R S T U V W X Y Z

Name: _____   Date: _____

O is for
Owl

Trace inside the cursive letter by following the arrows

Trace the cursive letters, then write your own.

_____

Trace inside the cursive letter by following the arrows

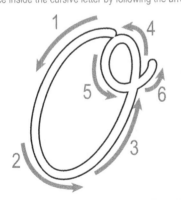

Trace the cursive letters, then write your own.

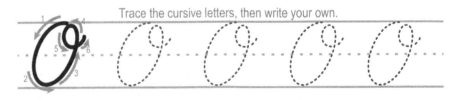

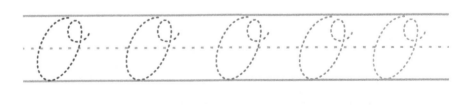

A B C D E F G H I J K L M N O P Q R S T U V W X Y Z

Name: _____   Date: _____

P is for

Panda

Trace inside the cursive letter by following the arrows

Trace the cursive letters, then write your own.

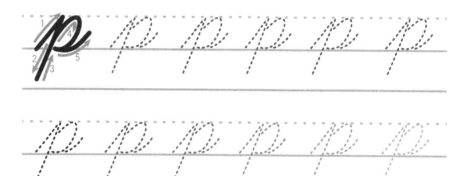

Trace inside the cursive letter by following the arrows

Trace the cursive letters, then write your own.

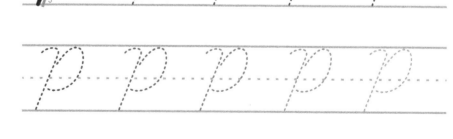

A B C D E F G H I J K L M N O **P** Q R S T U V W X Y Z

Name: _____   Date: _____

Q is for

Quail

Trace inside the cursive letter by following the arrows

Trace the cursive letters, then write your own.

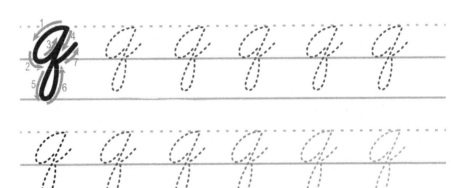

Trace inside the cursive letter by following the arrows

Trace the cursive letters, then write your own.

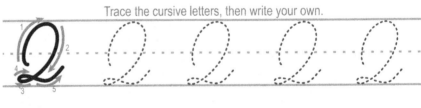

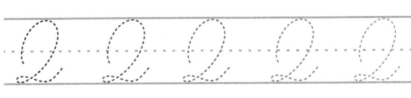

A B C D E F G H I J K L M N O P **Q** R S T U V W X Y Z

Name: _____   Date: _____

Trace inside the cursive letter by following the arrows

Trace the cursive letters, then write your own.

R is for Rabbit

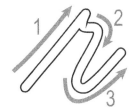

Trace inside the cursive letter by following the arrows

Trace the cursive letters, then write your own.

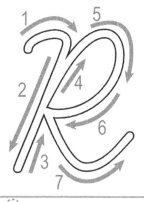

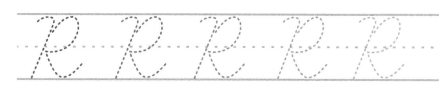

A B C D E F G H I J K L M N O P Q R S T U V W X Y Z

Name: _____   Date: _____

S is for Squirrel

Trace inside the cursive letter by following the arrows

Trace the cursive letters, then write your own.

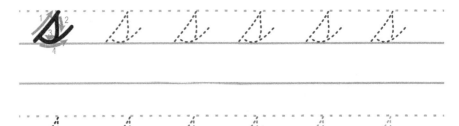

Trace inside the cursive letter by following the arrows

Trace the cursive letters, then write your own.

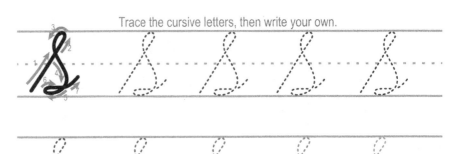

A B C D E F G H I J K L M N O P Q R **S** T U V W X Y Z

Name: _____   Date: _____

*T is for
Tiger*

Trace inside the cursive letter by following the arrows

Trace the cursive letters, then write your own.

Trace inside the cursive letter by following the arrows

Trace the cursive letters, then write your own.

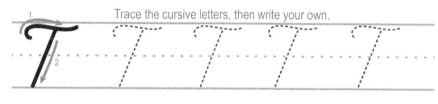

A B C D E F G H I J K L M N O P Q R S **T** U V W X Y Z

Name: _____   Date: _____

U is for

Unicorn

Trace inside the cursive letter by following the arrows

Trace the cursive letters, then write your own.

Trace inside the cursive letter by following the arrows

Trace the cursive letters, then write your own.

A B C D E F G H I J K L M N O P Q R S T U V W X Y Z

Name: _____ Date: _____

Trace inside the cursive letter by following the arrows

V is for

Vulture

Trace the cursive letters, then write your own.

Trace inside the cursive letter by following the arrows

Trace the cursive letters, then write your own.

A B C D E F G H I J K L M N O P Q R S T U **V** W X Y Z

Name: _____   Date: _____

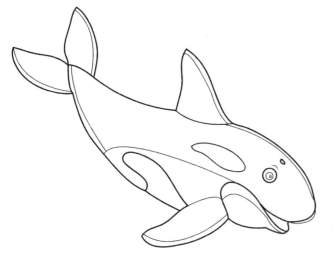

W is for

Whale

Trace inside the cursive letter by following the arrows

Trace the cursive letters, then write your own.

Trace inside the cursive letter by following the arrows

Trace the cursive letters, then write your own.

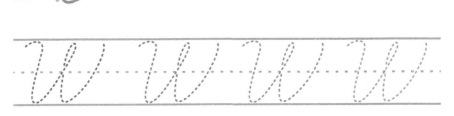

A B C D E F G H I J K L M N O P Q R S T U V **W** X Y Z

Name: _____   Date: _____

Trace inside the cursive letter by following the arrows

Trace the cursive letters, then write your own.

Trace inside the cursive letter by following the arrows

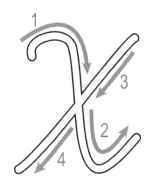

Trace the cursive letters, then write your own.

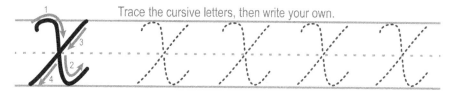

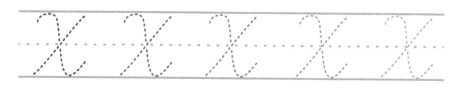

A B C D E F G H I J K L M N O P Q R S T U V W **X** Y Z

Name: _____   Date: _____

Y is for Yak

Trace inside the cursive letter by following the arrows

Trace the cursive letters, then write your own.

Trace inside the cursive letter by following the arrows

Trace the cursive letters, then write your own.

A B C D E F G H I J K L M N O P Q R S T U V W X **Y** Z

Name: _____

Date: _____

$\mathcal{Z}$ is for

Zebra

Trace inside the cursive letter by following the arrows

Trace the cursive letters, then write your own.

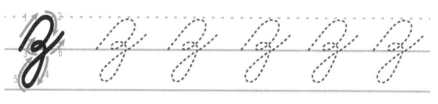

Trace inside the cursive letter by following the arrows

Trace the cursive letters, then write your own.

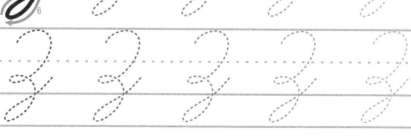

A B C D E F G H I J K L M N O P Q R S T U V W X Y **Z**

a b c d e f g h i j k l m

n o p q r s t u v w x

y z

a b c d e f g h i j k l m

n o p q r s t u v w x

y z

a b c d e f g h i j k l m

n o p q r s t u v w x

y z

a b c d e f g h i j k l m

n o p q r s t u v w x

y z

a b c d e f g h i j k l m

n o p q r s t u v w x

y z

a b c d e f g h i j k l m

n o p q r s t u v w x

y z

A B C D E F G H I

J K L M N O P Q R

S T U V W X Y Z

A B C D E F G H I

J K L M N O P Q R

S T U V W X Y Z

A B C D E F G H I

J K L M N O P Q R

S T U V W X Y Z

A B C D E F G H I

J K L M N O P Q R

S T U V W X Y Z

A B C D E F G H I

J K L M N O P Q R

S T U V W X Y Z

A B C D E F G H I

J K L M N O P Q R

S T U V W X Y Z

Name: _____   Date: _____

Aa Bb Cc Dd Ee Ff Gg

Hh Ii Jj Kk Ll Mm

Nn Oo Pp Qq Rr Ss Tt

Uu Vv Ww Xx Yy Zz

Aa Bb Cc Dd Ee Ff Gg

Hh Ii Jj Kk Ll Mm

Nn Oo Pp Qq Rr Ss Tt

Uu Vv Ww Xx Yy Zz

Name:

Date:

Aa Bb Cc Dd Ee Ff Gg

Hh Ii Jj Kk Ll Mm

Nn Oo Pp Qq Rr Ss Tt

Uu Vv Ww Xx Yy Zz

Aa Bb Cc Dd Ee Ff Gg

Hh Ii Jj Kk Ll Mm

Nn Oo Pp Qq Rr Ss Tt

Uu Vv Ww Xx Yy Zz

Name: _____   Date: _____

Part 2:

Two letter words

Trace and write the words.

Use the blank practice page to write
on your own at the end.

You are
AMAZING!

am am am am am

an an an an an

be be be be be

by by by by by

do do do do do

go go go go go

hi hi hi hi hi

he he he he he

it it it it it

if if if if if

be be be be be

me me me me me

my my my my my

no no no no no

of of of of of

on on on on on

pa pa pa pa pa

pi pi pi pi pi

so so so so so

to to to to to

Name: _____ Date: _____

Part 3:

Three Letter Words

Trace the words and practice writing them in the remaining space!

Use the blank practice page to write on your own at the end.

You are AWESOME!

and and and and

are are are are are

bat bat bat bat bat

box box box box

can can can can can

cow cow cow cow cow

dad dad dad dad dad

dog dog dog dog dog

eat eat eat eat eat

eye eye eye eye eye

fan fan fan fan fan

for for for for for

get get get get get

got got got got got

hat hat hat hat hat

hot hot hot hot hot

ink ink ink ink ink

its its its its its

joy joy joy joy joy

jug jug jug jug jug

key key key key key

kit kit kit kit kit

leg leg leg leg leg

kid kid kid kid kid

map map map map map

mom mom mom

not not not not not

menu menu menu menu

oun oun oun oun

off off off off off

pig pig pig pig pig

pen pen pen pen

qua qua qua qua qua

nat nat nat nat nat

ned ned ned ned ned

tea tea tea tea tea

sky sky sky sky sky

tie tie tie tie tie

toe toe toe toe toe

urn urn urn urn

use use use use use

nan nan nan nan

net net net net net

who who who who

why why why why

Name: _____   Date: _____

yum yum yum

you you you you

gip gip gip gip gip

goo goo goo goo goo

Write your own three letter words here:

Name: _____ Date: _____

Part 4:

Four Letter Words

Trace the words and practice writing them in the remaining space!

Use the blank practice page to write on your own at the end.

Great Going!

aunt aunt aunt aunt

away away away

bird bird bird bird

boat boat boat boat

care care care care

cool cool cool cool

deer deer deer deer

down down down

easy easy easy easy

even even even even

fork fork fork fork

from from from from

girl girl girl girl

gone gone gone gone

have have have have

help   help   help   help

idea   idea   idea   idea

iron   iron   iron   iron

joke   joke   joke   joke

just   just   just   just

kite kite kite kite

know know know

land land land

lock lock lock lock

mine mine mine mine

more more more

nest nest nest nest

nose nose nose nose

okay okay okay okay

over over over over

pair pair pair pair

post post post post

quad quad quad quad

quiz quiz quiz quiz

rain rain rain rain

ring ring ring ring

ship ship ship ship

soup soup soup soup

team team team team

they they they they

Name: _____ Date: _____

undo undo undo undo

unit unit unit unit

nose nose nose nose

nest nest nest nest

went went went went

with with with with

nmas nmas nmas

nnay nnay nnay nnay

yard yard yard yard

year year year year

geno geno geno geno

goom goom goom

Name: _____ Date: _____

Part 5:
Connecting Uppercase Letters

Trace the dotted words,
then write the words in the remaining space.

Use the blank practice page to write
on your own at the end.

You are
brilliant!

Am Am Am Am

Amy Amy Amy Amy

Bat Bat Bat Bat

Be Be Be Be

Can Can Can Can

These uppercase letters connect to lowercase letters: A C E G H J K L M N Q R S U X Y Z
These uppercase letters do not connect to lowercase letters: B D F I O P T V W

Name: _____   Date: _____

Cup   Cup   Cup   Cup

Do   Do   Do   Do

Dig   Dig   Dig   Dig

Eat   Eat   Eat   Eat

Elk   Elk   Elk   Elk

These uppercase letters connect to lowercase letters: A C E G H J K L M N Q R S U X Y Z
These uppercase letters do not connect to lowercase letters: B D F I O P T V W

Fin Fin Fin Fin

For For For For

Go Go Go Go

Get Get Get Get

Hi Hi Hi Hi

These uppercase letters connect to lowercase letters: A C E G H J K L M N Q R S U X Y Z
These uppercase letters do not connect to lowercase letters: B D F I O P T V W

Hen Hen Hen Hen

If If If If

It It It It

Jet Jet Jet Jet

Jug Jug Jug Jug

These uppercase letters connect to lowercase letters: A C E G H J K L M N Q R S U X Y Z

These uppercase letters do not connect to lowercase letters: B D F I O P T V W

Keg Keg Keg Keg

Kit Kit Kit Kit

Let Let Let Let

Log Log Log Log

May May May May

These uppercase letters connect to lowercase letters: A C E G H J K L M N Q R S U X Y Z
These uppercase letters do not connect to lowercase letters: B D F I O P T V W

Menu Menu Menu Menu

Net Net Net Net

Nod Nod Nod Nod

Oak Oak Oak Oak

Owl Owl Owl Owl

These uppercase letters connect to lowercase letters: A C E G H J K L M N Q R S U X Y Z
These uppercase letters do not connect to lowercase letters: B D F I O P T V W

Name: _____ Date: _____

Pair Pair Pair Pair

Pet Pet Pet Pet

Quill Quill Quill Quill

Quit Quit Quit Quit

Rep Rep Rep Rep

These uppercase letters connect to lowercase letters: A C E G H J K L M N Q R S U X Y Z
These uppercase letters do not connect to lowercase letters: B D F I O P T V W

Rug Rug Rug Rug

Say Say Say Say

Son Son Son Son

Tap Tap Tap Tap

Toy Toy Toy Toy

These uppercase letters connect to lowercase letters: A C E G H J K L M N Q R S U X Y Z
These uppercase letters do not connect to lowercase letters: B D F I O P T V W

Ugh Ugh Ugh Ugh

Used Used Used Used

Vest Vest Vest Vest

Vote Vote Vote Vote

Web Web Web Web

These uppercase letters connect to lowercase letters: A C E G H J K L M N Q R S U X Y Z
These uppercase letters do not connect to lowercase letters: B D F I O P T V W

Name: Date:

Wig Wig Wig Wig

Xenon Xenon Xenon

Xylem Xylem Xylem

Yak Yak Yak Yak

Yard Yard Yard Yard

These uppercase letters connect to lowercase letters: A C E G H J K L M N Q R S U X Y Z
These uppercase letters do not connect to lowercase letters: B D F I O P T V W

Zebra   Zebra   Zebra

Zeal Zeal Zeal Zeal

Practice writing your own words here:

These uppercase letters connect to lowercase letters: A C E G H J K L M N Q R S U X Y Z
These uppercase letters do not connect to lowercase letters: B D F I O P T V W

Name: _____   Date: _____

Part 6:
Numbers

Trace the dotted numbers and number words, then write them in the remaining space.

Use the blank practice page to write on your own at the end.

Fantastic!

Name: Date:

1 1 1 1

2 2 2 2

3 3 3 3

4 4 4 4

5 5 5 5

Numbers

6   6   6

7   7   7

8   8   8

9   9   9

10   10   10

Numbers

1 2 3 4 5 6 7 8 9 10

1 2 3 4 5 6 7 8 9 10

1 2 3 4 5 6 7 8 9 10

1 2 3 4 5 6 7 8 9 10

Numbers

One One

One

Two Two

Two

Three Three

Three

Four Four

Four

Five Five

Five

Number Words

Six Six

Six

Seven Seven

Seven

Eight Eight

Eight

Nine Nine

Nine

Ten Ten

Ten

Number Words

One Two Three Four

Five Six Seven Eight

Nine Ten

One Two Three Four

Five Six Seven Eight

Nine Ten

One Two Three Four

Five Six Seven Eight

Nine Ten

Name: _____   Date: _____

One Two Three Four

Five Six Seven Eight

Nine Ten

One Two Three Four

Five Six Seven Eight

Nine Ten

One Two Three Four

Five Six Seven Eight

Nine Ten

Number Words

Name: Date:

1 - One   1 - One

2 - Two   2 - Two

3 - Three   3 - Three

4 - Four   4 - Four

5 - Five   5 - Five

6 - Six   6 - Six

7 - Seven   7 - Seven

8 - Eight   8 - Eight

9 - Nine   9 - Nine

10 - Ten   10 - Ten

Number Words

10 – Ten

20 – Twenty

30 – Thirty

40 – Forty

50 – Fifty

60 – Sixty

70 – Seventy

80 – Eighty

90 – Ninety

100 – Hundred

Number Words

Name: _____   Date: _____

Part 7:
Sentences

Trace the dotted sentences, pangrams, jokes and riddles and then practice writing them on your own.

We will now practice writing the sentences using a smaller letter size.

Use your best handwriting!

Name:

Date:

I love my family.

I love my family.

He likes to play.

He likes to play.

A bug is on the rug.

A bug is on the rug.

Write your own sentences here:

Name: _____   Date: _____

The dog ran home.

The dog ran home.

I see a school bus.

I see a school bus.

She likes to draw.

She likes to draw.

Write your own sentences here:

Name: _____ Date: _____

I like the color red.

I like the color red.

I can read and write.

I can read and write.

Look at the big man.

Look at the big man.

Write your own sentences here:

Name: _____   Date: _____

My name is

I am ___ years old.

I like to

My best friend is

Practice writing your own sentences here:

Complete the sentences.

Name: Date:

The quick brown fox

jumps over a lazy dog.

How quickly daft

jumping zebras vex.

Write your own Pangram here:

Pangram: A pangram is a sentence that contains every letter of the alphabet at least once. Practice these fun lines.

Name: Date:

Sphinx of black quartz, judge my vow!

The five boxing wizards jump quickly.

Write your own Pangram here:

Pangram: A pangram is a sentence that contains every letter of the alphabet at least once. Practice these fun lines.

Name: _____   Date: _____

Both fickle dwarves

jinx my pig quiz.

Fix problem quickly

with galvanized jets.

Write your own Pangram here:

Pangram: A pangram is a sentence that contains every letter of the alphabet at least once. Practice these fun lines.

What belongs to you but

others use more?

Your name.

What do you call a

sleeping bull?

A bulldozer!

What goes up when the

rain comes down?

An umbrella.

Write your own joke or riddle here:

What kind of shoes do

spies wear?

Sneakers.

What vehicle has four

wheels and flies?

A garbage truck.

How many pears grow

on a tree?

All of them.

Write your own joke or riddle here:

Name: _____   Date: _____

Why don't lobsters share?

They're shellfish.

Where do you learn to

make ice cream?

At sundae school.

What's orange and sounds

like a parrot?

A carrot!

Write your own joke or riddle here:

Name: Date:

Without geometry,

life is pointless.

What do you call a bear

with no teeth?

A gummy bear!

Want to hear my pizza

joke?

Never mind, it's too

cheesy.

Write your own joke or riddle here:

Name: Date:

How does a penguin

built it's house?

Igloos it together.

What rhymes with

orange?

No it doesn't.

Why don't scientists

trust Atoms?

They make up everything.

Write your own joke or riddle here:

What do you call an

alligator in a nest?

An investigator!

When's the best time to

go to the dentist?

Tooth hurt-y.

What do you call cheese

that isn't yours?

Nacho Cheese.

Write your own joke or riddle here:

Name: Date:

Name: Date:

Cursive writing
Completed ✔

CONGRATULATIONS!
You are a
CHAMPION!

Celebrate, get creative
and design your own comic

✔ Get it Today

Celebrate your Success!

Share the Joy!

Feel Great Everyday!

Write to me at **sujatha.lalgudi@gmail.com** with the subject:
Jojo Cursive along with **your kid's name** to receive:

- Additional practice worksheets.
- A name tracing worksheet so your kid can practice writing their own name.
- An Award Certificate in Color to gift your kid!

Congratulations

Writing Super Star
Awarded to

_____

For _____

Date _____   **Signed** _____

Made in the USA
Las Vegas, NV
10 September 2022